Coral Gables

America's Finest Suburb

Miami, Florida

An Interpretation By
Marjory Stoneman Douglas

*A Great
American
City-Region*

F YOU HAD never heard of Coral Gables, but thrilled with some vast sunset, had adventured westward from Miami on that Ta-Miami Trail which marches clean across Florida from the Atlantic to the Gulf of Mexico, and had come upon a tremendous gateway, revealing to the southward a city like an artist's dream set in a great open garden, you would go through that gateway, drawn by an urge to know more. You couldn't help it. But when you had followed the boulevards sweeping like great ribbons through the whole 3500 acres, through the actual soil and structure of a man's vision, when you had been absorbed and uplifted by that sense of far-flung design which makes one whole of superb sky, crystal light and marching green acres with roads and groves and trees and colorful houses and golf links and more houses and shops and tennis courts and gardens and hotels, you would have learned more than the fact that it was called Coral Gables. You would know also that you had seen the working out of a new idea. For it is now certain that Coral Gables has become, not only a splendid adventure in creative development, but the first thoroughly established city-region in the United States.

We are accustomed, in this country, to ugly cities. The great American superstition is that ugliness is a practical necessity for American cities. We pride ourselves upon organizing ability, on our engineering ability, on our practical far-sightedness. Yet in the matter of creating cities to live in we have only two methods. The first is the cow-path method

Interior of Coral Gables Office, Merrick Building, Miami

which seems to believe that man cannot be more efficient for himself than a wandering animal. The other is the engineer method, which is simply that of snapping down a ruler on a map and criss crossing it with straight lines, right angled, no matter what the configuration of the land, the transportation problems, the living necessities of the people. Both these methods result in cities as hideous and as inefficient as a bad dream. And our impractical and stupid manner of disassociating a city from the country around it, as if it were still a medieval fortress, brings it about that our modern cities are not only hideous and inefficient, but huge and bloated and chaotic; they shut out their people from all the joyous natural advantages of the country, which provides the absolute essentials of exercise and air and gardens which lie at the basis of human health. Not even the most ingenious park system has ever been able to make up for this lack.

In the few cases, like Washington, where a city plan was made before the city was built, the planners did achieve a civic design, but so coldly and so formally that the neighborhood life of people was almost forgotten. A park system and a distant vista of great buildings cannot make up for the lack of consideration.

That is why Coral Gables is so remarkable. It is a city, not at all politically so, but a city in such intimate relation with the region in which it is built that it is more like a great garden set with houses, a park where all the people can live to their best capacities, than a city in the old sense. It is not a city in a region, or a region in a city, but literally that

[4]

A place where folks can live sanely, healthfully, zestfully, valuably

new phrase, a city-region, the most modern, the most far-seeing method which has yet been found to preserve the right relation between man and his work and his play and his environment.

For new ideas we must have new definitions. Coral Gables is a new idea. Therefore the definition "city-region" has been shaped to fit it. The basis of that is the "region" which geographers use to mean a section of country which has the same natural characteristics. We might have a river region or a mountain region or a valley region. In the case of Coral Gables it is a pineland region. But the old idea of region was merely rough, undeveloped country. You couldn't call Coral Gables that, because it is a place developed to the highest degree for people to live in, more or less as a city is. So when we combine the idea of "region" which means country, and "city" which is where men live, we got a better thing by calling it a "city-region." That is, the whole great acreage is developed as a city would be as far as buildings go, but so placed that the whole countryside becomes a wide, green and gracious city, and the city becomes a combination of park and garden and country expanse.

Any brief glimpse of Coral Gables gives one this splendid stimulating sense of discovery, the exhilarating realization that here at last wisdom and art and craftsmanship have met the age-old problem of how best shall a man live. When George E. Merrick, the man whose dream Coral Gables was and still is, visioned the thing which he wanted, he must have felt infinitely sickened of the old cities. He had seen cities built for men to make money in, ugly barren

[6]

The Country Club with charming Spanish tower

working cities, which produce bitter lives and cramped children. Hell, Shelley said, was a city like London. The working cities of the north and west are also like it. Mr. Merrick had seen cities built for men to spend money in, chaotic, disturbed, tawdry cities, cheapening the life of the whole region where they took their mushroom growth. But he had seen very few built primarily for men to live in. Yet how immeasurably the city where a man lives conditions everything about him, his health, his work, his pleasures, the welfare and the future of his family, all his thoughts and his happiness. We shut our eyes, in this country, to all this, under the old pioneer necessity of making the best of it.

But Mr. Merrick had an idea of making the best of it with a difference. So he laid out his region, where the gates and towers and roofs of his city were to be, with the feeling first of all that this was to be a place where a man and his family could live to the fullest degree possible, sanely, healthfully, zestfully, valuably. He built Coral Gables to be a city-region whose citizens would be rich in all the things which make a man's life interesting and worthwhile.

Coral Gables begins with the sky. The sky, in Coral Gables, is literally its third limit. After you have stood on a street corner or a front lawn or the golf links and let your eyes and the flight of your mind carry you up the tremendous dome of the sky, you wonder why mountainous regions are called, "The Land of the Sky." Only here, where the great reaches of earth are so open that you can see from one low horizon to the other; only here where the tropic blue stretches above you, a blue deeper and more dazzling than

The pines stand guard for the rich green of the fruit groves

any other in America, and where the majestic Gulf clouds like sculptured snow come drifting slowly over before the trade wind that makes the whole air salt sweet with distant sea and vital and stimulating with movement, do you realize what a South Florida sky is really like. And when you stand awestruck, as everywhere at the hour of sunset you see people standing, to watch the sunset exploding all over the sky in such marvels of gold and bronze and molten copper, such changing bursts of scarlet and lavender as you have never seen before, you will realize why the sunset hour is an event in Coral Gables. There are stars, also, just beyond the treetops, and moons, huge, glowing tropic moons, that turn the air into silver and the links and roads into pools and streaks of silver, and the palms and pines and groves into black magic touched with silver and the night to witchery, through which the lanterns and street lights make more enchantment and the music from the country club dances, drifting between, into the horns of a realized city of delight.

Sky and air is the first requisite to human living. Then comes the quality and nature of the broad earth itself. Years ago, before Miami was much of a settlement, Coral Gables was a great pine forest, mile after mile after mile of those rare and beautiful trees which you find in no other place in America except South Florida, the true tropical Carribbean pine. Then when Mr. Merrick's father first cleared pineland for his groves of orange and grapefruit, the pines' high and lacey ranks stood guard for the deep rich green of the fruit groves, groves which added gust after gust of exquisite perfume to the pine-sweet air at blossoming time and lit the

[10]

Where lofty palms stretch a dark arm over the loveliest homes

shade with pale gold clusters in deep-fruited winters. So that the pine tree and the orange tree are the first tree-symbols of Coral Gables, witnesses to the bounty of the dark soil.

Everywhere possible the pines have been left. Clear around the full circle of the horizon, behind the farthest houses and over-topping them, the piney ranks march, an etched mural decoration linking earth and sky. A sunset is a greater splendor because its crimson bursts behind their black intricacies and moonlight is more magic because of them. They are the guardians of great houses. They stretch a dark arm over the smallest home. They make parkways significant with loveliness and the long curving roads fit for many cameras. And the groves of orange and grapefruit, sturdier trees and more prolific each year, are equally everywhere, making cool shady avenues of streets and bringing promise of luscious breakfast to housewives, who can pick their own fruit from their own porches. But to be really Floridian, really tropic, Mr. Merrick added a third tree, the incomparable coconut palm. Huge-fronded, lifting their superb curves in groups about tile-roof buildings, making a tropic delight of swimming pool and dance floor, the coconut palms grow freely. They were transplanted here bodily from the Florida keys, only two years or so ago and now are perfectly at home. The palm, the pine, the citrus fruit, these three are the dominating tree friends of Coral Gables.

Of course there are dozens of other varieties of trees. The strange sea grape grows in many a plaza, there are streets of sturdy pithecolobiums and lebbeks and eucalyptus and

The Venetian pool, that wonder of shimmering blue and green

Santa Marias, all well known tropic trees, rare to the eyes of the northerner. The beauty of their leaf and branch and shade will be added to that of palm and orange and pine as the well stocked Coral Gables nurseries attest.

The land was rich pine land, with a few hammocks of jungle growth, where Mr. Merrick chose to create his city-region. Level for the most part, it has many little lifts and rises, gentle slopes, rock ridges where a strata was turned, and an infinite sense of distance. No engineer ever set ruler callously to map to criss-cross these streets. A few main boulevards sweep straightly, as main arteries of traffic from Miami, from Coconut Grove and from neighboring county roads. But the rest are laid out as the land required, curving easily, with wide parkways, and opening into great open plazas, walled and arched, set with pools of water, a fit background for the most carefully studied landscape gardening and already chosen spots for the better type of motion pictures. The whole system of roads and boulevards and plazas is equally a delight to the eye of the artist or the wheel of the motorist. As a consequence, to drive about Coral Gables is constantly to be discovering new charms of roadways, new vistas of great distance, new tunnels of green which open out to light flooded plazas, new curving perspectives of trees and charming roofs and great lifts of sky.

Not only the looks of things were regarded, of course, although the attractiveness of the streets of any town are, like that of a child, the sign of health. The roads are built for heavy traffic, for a constant stream of automobiles, and

It is such an inn-yard as Shakespeare wrote, "Romeo and Juliet" to be played in

so shrewdly that in all Coral Gables there are no dangerous corners, no death traps. Nor does one waste time driving about them. Their planning takes account of the fact that for driving in a city curves are more often the shortest distance between two points.

Of course, the secret of the matter of roads, and of all buildings here, is that Coral Gables had, not just a city plan, but before the first road was laid out or the first house built, which amounted really to a regional plan. The whole 3500 acres was taken into consideration, the nature and condition of the terrain, the possibilities of the soil, the location, in regard to Miami, the nearest avenues of transportation, and all the types and characteristics of the future development. So when great open plazas were laid out at the intersections of many of the main boulevards, plazas with seductive Spanish names like Segovia and Ponce de Leon, the beginnings of the architectural city were made. These plazas serve the double purpose of solving traffic problems and furnishing, with their sweeping, sunbaked walls and dripping pools, their wealth of vines and their mellow suggestion of an age-old leisure, the keynote for all later structures.

But the matter of planting did not end with laying out the streets and regional highways. The future city had to be zoned. It is the folly and ignorance of old cities that allows a factory to be put up in the open space of a residential district, or shops to encroach upon schools and playgrounds, or the tumult of industry upon churches, libraries and hospitals. In Coral Gables there are no factories, but there are industries. People work, in Coral Gables, better because

Plazas with a wealth of foliage and their mellow suggestion of age-old leisure

of the light and the air, the convenience and the beauty. So a business zone was laid out, centering about a business hotel. The remarkable printing plant of Col. Parker, the maker of building blocks, the carpenter shop, the plumbers and cement workers, have their own district, which is equally as attractive as any other, the parkways as carefully kept, the shrubs and vines on the charming buildings just as well cared for. There is the shopping district, next to the business district, and that is also unique, a great colonnaded block, with splendid orange and brown and yellow and dull blue awnings, where the people of Coral Gables do their shopping conveniently and in no time at all, because there is no necessity for hunting about from street to street for scattered stores. That neither business nor industry needs to be hideous is one of the great modern city-building truths which Mr. Merrick has demonstrated.

After the first plan, after the roads were built and the zones determined on, after the excellent water system and the electric lighting plant, there came the actual question of the houses. The architecture of Coral Gables is unique, from the point of view of all other places in America. The geography, the climate, the tropical horticulture and tropical characteristics of South Florida are matters which have nothing in common with the west or north or the old south. The straight levels of the land, the brilliance of the light, the unique backgrounds of tropical trees and sky demands an architecture which is not imitative of other forms or suited to other places. To be right, it must answer local problems of living. To allow here an old Colonial imitation, there

Thresholds of delight through which sunlight and moonlight fall meltingly

a pseudo-Tudor, next door a rococo horror of the early American pullman type or a California bungalow with great, clumsy earthquake pillars, on these streets which in themselves made a perfect whole, would have destroyed everything. It would no longer be Coral Gables.

It was determined first of all, therefore, that a modified type of Spanish architecture, thoroughly adapted to local needs, should be the style of the whole. And the keynote was first struck, and most impressively, on the great gateways which, on the Ta-Miami Trail, on Douglas Road, at the Country Club entrance, lead the world into Coral Gables. They are made of native rock, that interesting coral-like substance which mellows under the blows of the tropic sun to the color of old ivory and orange-blossom honey. This rock was to be the basic building material, no imported alien stuff, but the foundation rock of the region itself. To use it properly in the gateways, Spanish masons were brought in from Cuba, men who were familiar with the idea that everything connected with the every day living of people should be beautiful and worthy. With this rock and these men Mr. Denman Fink, the artist-in-chief, went out to build the gateways. They were not drawn on paper. They grew directly in stone, the massive walls, the wide great arches that frame so perfectly the distant vistas. Granada gateway, on the Trail, has somewhat the atmosphere of old Seville, but better yet, it is the interpretation of South Florida, in native rock, in strength, beauty, practical value, and a sense of high purpose for the future. They make the most perfect background for great coconut palms, for the

Wide, great arches that frame so perfectly the distant vistas

creamy white blossoms of yucca, for the rioting blooms of the flame vine and the deeper purples of bougainvillea. The future of Coral Gables is to be read in each one of them.

After the gateways and plazas, the houses and buildings grew. And literally, they seem to grow, because each house, each shop, each structure, has the sense of fitting gracefully into its background, that sense of intimate belonging which come only of loving forethought. They have none of that look of packing boxes scattered over an empty lot, which so many new houses have. Nor is any one house in a street permitted to be out of key, inharmonious, with the others. Each in its ample lawn, of infinitely charming variety, are built to complete and enhance the others. In spite of their individual treatment and detail, they are related.

But such a wealth of detail. To ride slowly up and down a street, attracted first by its total harmony, and then by the desire of studying closely the individual houses, is constantly to discover new charms. The small houses are as carefully worked out as the larger ones, the veranda, arches and doorways as genuinely artistic, with everywhere some touch of decoration, some group of windows, some fascinating line of roof and wall and chimney which indicate the possibility of gracious living within. The larger residences have that same sense, heightened perhaps, but only in proportion. Their doorways are thresholds of delight, leading by columns and arches through which sunlight and moonlight fall meltingly, into deep verandas and tiled patios where life in South Florida flows scented and leisurely and

Studying closely individual homes is constantly to discover new charms

infinitely varied. Their great rooms are fit backgrounds for furniture and hangings redolent of conquistadores and armadas, but by reason of their great windows, are ante-chambers to the sky and air. Much architectural cunning has gone into these houses, for of course they must satisfy the modern housewife's desire for household efficiency, as well as lovely living. The ubiquitous electric lights are not allowed to be too blatant. The shinning plumbing and kitchen fittings, the hot and cold water, the electric plugs, the deep closets and the handy shelves are there. They are merely allowed not to obtrude. One can be sure they are there, and live forgetful of them.

Of all the details of the houses, the roof tiles are the most noticeable and the most immediately fascinating. Roofs are always so much more important than people think they are. The roof lines of a country always tell you tales about the country itself, of snow and sleet, of mountain avalanches, of possible earthquakes, or of great reaches of sun and air, such as this. Nothing but tile would have done for Coral Gables, tile of the mellowest to set against the background of lacey pines and lifting cloud dazzle. But not the glarey shinyness of new commercially made tile, in ugly reds which would swear at the purple of bougainvillea or bottle green to put out of countenance the soft greens of palm and vine. Nothing would do but old Spanish tile, hand-made, with all the lovable variety of old things tile that would weave grey and dull brown and soft moss green and old umber together into a roof covering as friendly as the earth, related to wall-tone and rock-tone and tree-tone. From a distance each

Fascinating architectural features which indicate gracious living within

roof melts and blends with its neighbor, at different levels and different angles, picturesque, eternally satisfying. That was the only possible tile for Coral Gables. They had to get it, no matter under what difficulties. So they found it in Havana, ship loads of it, old hand-made tile brought from Spain in ancient high-pooped galleons in the days when buccaneers made the Spanish Main a great adventure and the grandees rustled their silks and clashed their steel in the first Havana. Roofs of crumbling convents, of old houses being torn down to make room for new streets, ancient bodegas and prisons and barracks, gave up their tiles to make Coral Gables' charm unique. In Havana they would have been destroyed. In South Florida, they come into their own again.

If the color of the roof tiles was important, how much the coloring of the houses themselves must have been considered. For after line and mass and harmonious relation, you are always conscious, in Coral Gables, of the beauty of color. With the warm cream and amber of the tinted cement and native rock, there are window casings of dull blue or sage green, timbers touched with design in chrome yellow and Italian blue and Chinese red, touches of cool vermillion and sienna and emerald about a gable end, hints of burnt orange and that purple which is the color of new grapes, in a doorway. It does not flaunt at you. You recognize it only as a part of the whole. But what a part.

For after all, this is a country keyed to color. The blazing sky and the white light and the distant reaches of grey-green demand it, can hold it properly. Just as the Greeks and the Latins of the Mediterranean throw living

Columns and arches where life flows scented and leisurely and infinitely varied

color against the blue of their skies which are not half so deep or so glowing as these South Florida ones, so the architects and artists of Coral Gables use their colors. The stucco houses themselves are washed with color, a rich color as the under coat, and the second, a light one, often of another, but blending, as a result, into something infinitely warm and textured and right for the shadows of trees and vines and clouds to make charming.

And finally, in the whole question of color, we come to the exclamation points, the awnings. As a rule no one pays much attention to awnings. The north knows them as something to shade a window which must be uninteresting and neutral to withstand rain and dust. But in Coral Gables, the awnings, as every other detail, are a fine art. They are necessary to a house, in the first place, not just to shade windows, but to spread over a patio or roof a high balcony or give the necessary protection to a colonnade or a loggia or a roof top garden. The whole awning color, carelessly chosen, could upset the color scheme of any house, could ruin the plan of a whole street. So the awnings were made the high lights of the whole plan, until every street, and every group of streets, is as splendidly harmonized as a great painting. You will see awnings striped with dull red and brown, on a cream colored house, with just one front awning shouting in warm henna. The next house will be in key with dull blue and lemon yellow, the next sage green striped with black, but the whole pattern like a cunningly woven tapestry. Any street gives that intense satisfaction which only color, lots of color, but always the right color, can give.

Roofs of crumbling convents gave up their tiles to make Coral Gables' charm

Of the individual buildings it is hard to choose because in each there is detail enough to make a separate chapter. There is the country club, for instance, with the charming Spanish tower and the round open air dance floor set in a coconut grove. There is the home of George Merrick, on a ridge among Caribbean pines, grey and mellow and lovely with a satisfying simplicity. There is the block of stores with the delightful colonnade. There is the new church and the high school and any number of residences such as Dr. Dammers', whose fine lines and mass are so noteworthy. One of the most fascinating is the hotel in the business district. It will eventually be only one of the smaller hotels, but what a joy it is. From the tiled courtyard and over-hanging, wooden-railed balconies, to the deep fireplaces, the leaded windows and the beamed ceilings, it is an inn both Spanish and Elizabethan, modern and of Coral Gables. You can see Francis Drake or some forgotten captain of the Armada swaggering about in high boots and gold lace, or Sancho Panza flirting with a chamber maid on the balcony. It is such an inn-yard as Shakespeare wrote "Romeo and Juliet" to be played in. Yet it is not even an imitation of a Spanish inn. It is the right adaption of an old charm to new ways of living and a new and unique setting. It is a fitting product of its region and of an architectural genius which know how to interpret it.

With such backgrounds, the life at Coral Gables moves. The silky green of the great golf links centres it, with all that means of air and wide view, health and interest and recreation. The tennis courts are everywhere, and everywhere

Each home has the sense of fitting gracefully into its background

available. And the Venetian pool, that wonder of shimmering blues and greens, stretches its cool expanse under the coconut palms, for the slim bodies of swimmers to curve to, or glide under to blue grottos, or lie basking lazily on the sun-dappled surface.

Churches, auditoriums, conservatories of music and galleries of art, schools and concert halls and lecture rooms, the life of the mind as well as the sanest and most delightful life of healthy bodies, all are here provided for. Beyond food, shelter and clothing, man has the need of work, play, love of his kind, and worship. For such living, in a region developed to the highest degree as city-in-country and country-in-city, Coral Gables contributes finely and completely. The people who are living and working and playing in Coral Gables are making it, not just a place, but a community, based on the common joy in their situation and their common belief in the possibilities of the future. They complete the idea which Mr. Merrick began, that idea which is more than city planning, more even than a great development. It is the idea that to build a city-region such as this and translate it into valuable and interesting living, is to have begun a higher kind of creative statesmanship, that statesmanship which recognizes that all human endeavor must first contribute to the furtherance of that supreme wealth of the people, life in abundance. That is what Coral Gables does.

PARKER ART PRINTING ASS'N.
CORAL GABLES, MIAMI, FLA

CPSIA information can be obtained
at www.ICGtesting.com
Printed in the USA
BVHW041153080322
630909BV00009B/207